Transport
Lorries

by Mari Schuh

a Capstone company — publishers for children

Raintree is an imprint of Capstone Global Library Limited, a company incorporated in England and Wales having its registered office at 264 Banbury Road, Oxford, OX2 7DY – Registered company number: 6695582

www.raintree.co.uk
myorders@raintree.co.uk

Text © Capstone Global Library Limited 2018
The moral rights of the proprietor have been asserted.

All rights reserved. No part of this publication may be reproduced in any form or by any means (including photocopying or storing it in any medium by electronic means and whether or not transiently or incidentally to some other use of this publication) without the written permission of the copyright owner, except in accordance with the provisions of the Copyright, Designs and Patents Act 1988 or under the terms of a licence issued by the Copyright Licensing Agency, Saffron House, 6–10 Kirby Street, London EC1N 8TS (www.cla.co.uk). Applications for the copyright owner's written permission should be addressed to the publisher.

Edited by Carrie Braulick Sheely
Designed by Lori Bye
Picture research by Wanda Winch
Production by Laura Manthe
Originated by Capstone Global Library Limited
Printed and bound in India

ISBN 978 1 4747 4429 4 (hardback)
21 20 19 18 17
10 9 8 7 6 5 4 3 2 1

ISBN 978 1 4747 4435 5 (paperback)
22 21 20 19 18
10 9 8 7 6 5 4 3 2 1

Durham County Council Libraries, Learning and Culture	
C0 3 74 93179 X0	
Askews & Holts	
J629	

British Library Cataloguing in Publication Data
A full catalogue record for this book is available from the British Library.

Acknowledgements
We would like to thank the following for permission to reproduce photographs: Alamy Stock Photo: South West Images Scotland, 7, Transport/Stephen Barnes, 8–9; Capstone Studio: Karon Dubke, 11; Dreamstime: Davidebner, 21; iStockphoto: 8c061bbf_466, 12–13; Shutterstock: Adrian Reynolds, cover, Kisan, steel design, Mario Pantelic, lines design, Mike Brake, 17, Paul J. Martin, 5, Robert J. Beyers II, 15, T. Sumaetho, zoom motion design, Tony Baggett, 19

Every effort has been made to contact copyright holders of material reproduced in this book. Any omissions will be rectified in subsequent printings if notice is given to the publisher.

All the internet addresses (URLs) given in this book were valid at the time of going to press. However, due to the dynamic nature of the internet, some addresses may have changed, or sites may have changed or ceased to exist since publication. While the author and publisher regret any inconvenience this may cause readers, no responsibility for any such changes can be accepted by either the author or the publisher.

Contents

On the road 4
Parts. 8
Types 12

Glossary 22
Find out more 23
Comprehension questions 24
Index 24

On the road

What's that noise?

A big lorry goes down the road.

Here it comes!

Lorries haul loads.

They can carry logs.

See them go!

Parts

Lorries have big engines.

They often use diesel fuel.

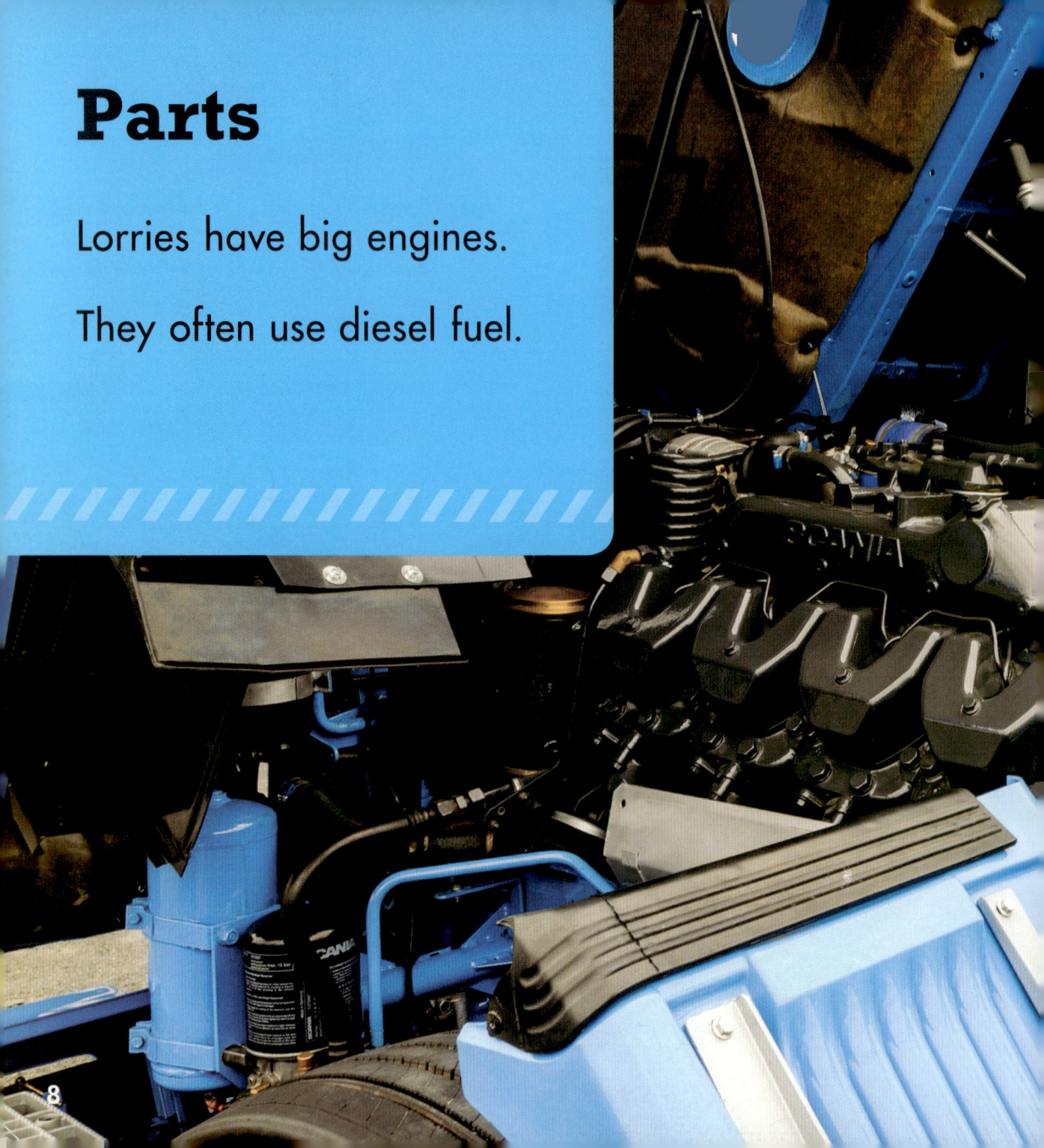

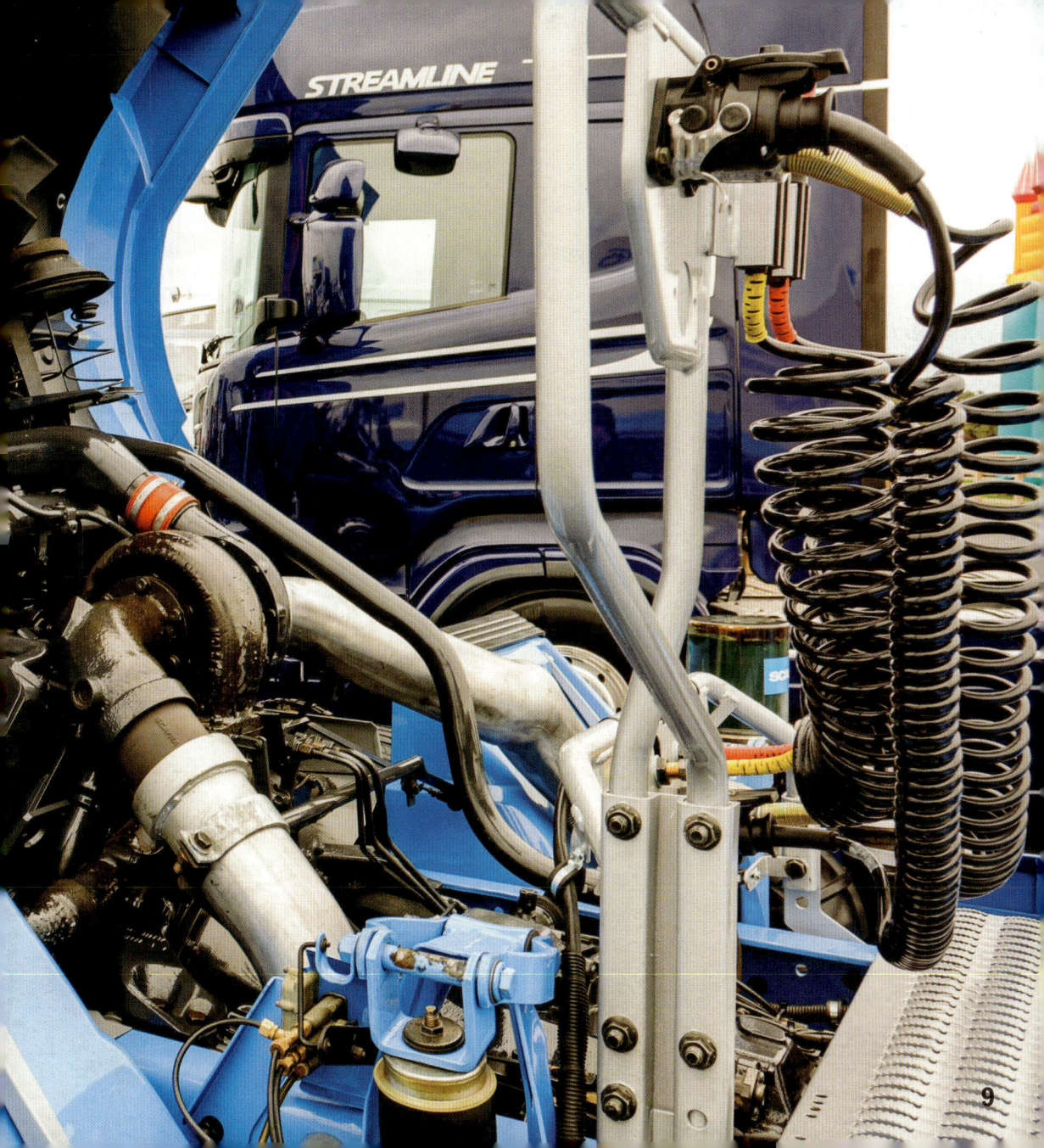

The cab is at the front.

The driver sits in the cab.

She starts the engine.

Let's go!

Types

A tanker is long.

It can hold milk or fuel

A dumper truck has a bed.

The bed holds heavy loads.

It tips up.

It dumps the load!

A fire engine puts out fires.

It has long hoses.

Whoosh!

They spray water.

A bin lorry is busy.

It picks up lots of rubbish.

It goes to the landfill.

Monster trucks have big wheels.

These trucks fly through the air.

They smash cars flat!

Glossary

bed back end of a dumper truck; the bed tips up to dump loads

cab area for a driver to sit in a large truck or machine

diesel fuel heavy fuel that burns to make power

engine machine in which fuel burns to provide power

haul pull or carry a load

landfill place where rubbish is buried

load anything that must be lifted and carried by a vehicle, person or machine

Find out more

Books

Big Machines Drive! (Big Machines), Catherine Veitch (Raintree, 2015)

Look Inside Things That Go (Usborne Look Inside) Rob Lloyd Jones (Usborne Publishing Ltd, 2013)

Machines on the Road (Machines at Work), Sian Smith (Raintree, 2014)

Trucks (Usborne Beginners), Katie Daynes (Usborne Publishing Ltd, 2007)

Websites

www.dkfindout.com/uk/search/transport/
Learn about different types of transport.

http://www.bbc.co.uk/education/clips/zj3myrd
Discover the type of fuel that lorries use.

Comprehension questions

1. Name two parts that trucks often have in common.

2. Why might people use trucks instead of other vehicles?

3. Name two ways that trucks can help people.

Index

bin lorry 18
cabs 10
drivers 10
dumper trucks 14
engines 8, 10
fire engine 16
fuel 8, 12
hoses 16

landfills 18
loads 6, 14
logs 6
milk 12
monster trucks 20
tankers 12
wheels 20